Expert

Secrets

Ed JC Smith

Expert Coach Secrets

Unlock Your Free Coaching Certification Course Now!

Scan the QR Code Below and Join Over 15,000 Coaches getting certified for FREE!

Get Certified for FREE (Valued at $5,000)

Become a Qualified Coach
Level Up Your Coaching Skills
Create the Impact You Want
Do What You Love

Don't Miss Out – Start Your Journey Today!

"You cannot solve a problem with the same level of thinking."

Albert Einstein

CONTENTS

INTRODUCTION

Ever since I started coaching, I had the idea of leading a very special, very high priced retreat for coaches.

Everywhere I looked, self-proclaimed coaching experts were running retreats and charging $5,000 to $20,000+, and they were getting plenty of coaches and aspiring coaches to pay.

Most of those running these retreats were one trick ponies, self-proclaimed gurus, marketing experts or motivational speakers. Few of them had my breadth and depth of coaching experience.

If they could get away with charging $5,000, $10,000, $15,000, I reasoned I could at least charge $10,000, right?

So that's what I did. I spoke to my business partner and he agreed to it too.

Three months later, we had everything in place and we'd sold 10 people to our coaching transformation retreat in Bali.

The only thing left was to come up with program content for the 10 days that would justify the investment of $10,000 that each attendee had invested.

What could I do with those coming that would be worth so much time and money?

It wasn't going to be easy.

Each one of them was different.

Some were beginner coaches. Many had been coaching for a number of years and some had over 10 years in the industry.

To make things more challenging, the markets they were coaching in ranged from business consulting, to anxiety, to relationships, to mindset, to health and fitness.

To make the retreat work for everyone I had to put something together that would be truly different.

I thought about it long and hard, but I couldn't come up with anything substantial.

So I called in my business partner and asked him what he thought.

And I said, "What is it that all coaches, regardless of what kind of industry they're in, want for themselves and their clients?"

"From what I'm seeing," my business partner said, "brand new coaches want to know how to get started and people who are already coaching want to know how they can level up."

Both answers sounded right to me.

"That's what we're going to do," I said. "I'm going to put together a program so that everyone who comes, whether they're a beginner, an intermediate, or even an experienced coach, will leave the retreat with a step by step to level up."

Despite their differences, all the coaches that attended the retreat all wanted the same thing.

They wanted to level up.

And guess what?

At the end of our time together, all of them said that they knew exactly what they needed to do in order to do that.

I was hugely grateful and proud of their transformations, knowing also what they could then do with others.

Half of them said they'd gotten their money's worth from the retreat after the first day. The rest on our last day together vocally committed to the specific actions they were going to take, or were already taking, to get to that next level.

Overall, their experience was worth far more than the $10,000 that each one of them had invested.

In this book, you will have access to all the concepts we covered at the retreat and many more that we didn't have time to cover.

If you read this book positively and with an open mind, you will get every strategy and skill you need to become an Expert Coach.

What you have to give is simply your commitment and your time.

Commitment is what every one of the attendees gave at the retreat, and those commitments we're enough to get all of them to become Expert Coaches.

Chapter 1

WHAT'S THE PURPOSE OF COACHING?

The purpose of coaching is to help your client out of a problem or pain and into a pleasure or desire.

That is the fundamental purpose of coaching.

But let's go a little bit more granular...

You're going to help your client to see a new view of life that is hidden from them and you're going to help your client to take responsibility for their life.

Our role is to discover through questions how the client perceives the problem and how they perceive being stuck in a view.

Our role is to ignite our client to dwell in the world of responsibility.

Our role is to guide our client to create a fulfilled life on their terms.

Note I say, "on their terms", not "on our terms".

It has to be on their terms.

You're going to help your client see a new view of life that they can't see and you're going to help them move further forward on their terms.

Your role is to help your client understand why they fell down the hole so they can increase their awareness and jump over the hole next time.

In order to do this, they have to be on board.

Consider this:

Spark + Fuel = Fire

The coach is the spark.

But without the client bringing the fuel, then there is no fire.

And so there has to be two in this.

Coaching is a dance, and it takes two to do a dance together.

Coaching is not a "do to" process.

People used to say to me, "Ed, do it to me."

"No," I would say, "we do it together."

Coaching is a "do with" process.

Without the client doing the work too, it will not happen.

Without you doing the work too, it will not happen.

Notice how much your client really wants the result.

If the client is not willing to partake in the work and if the coach is not willing to partake in the work, then we don't get the fire.

The coach brings the spark. Your client will bring the fuel. And then you have a fire.

Maybe the fuel's not ready yet...

Maybe it's been a bit dampened...

Maybe you need to dry it out...

The wood has to be in acceptance of becoming a fire in order to become a fire.

If it's in denial, then it won't set alight.

The wood has to want to create fire.

People used to say to me, "Do it to me, Ed. Make me better."

I would reply, "It will not happen without you doing the work too. You need to be invested one hundred percent into making this happen."

"To get the result, I will bring one hundred percent. However, if you bring ten percent, it will not happen."

As you transform someone's belief system as a by-product, their behaviours will transform also.

What someone believes about themselves will define their behaviours.

They will still need accountability.

They will still need to work to create that new possibility so that it stays.

They still need to do the daily training. And when they do, the transformation will stay.

When people say, "Ed, motivation doesn't last." I say, "Correct, it doesn't. Motivation doesn't last. Neither does brushing your teeth. You have to do it every day."

Transformation will not last if you do not do the work every day to maintain a transformed life.

Notice how much you want the transformation too...

Just like your client, as you put more in, you are going to get massive transformation in yourself through your coaching.

Your client results are going to be a by-product.

But your life's going to rapidly change every step of the way.

The more expert you become as a coach, the more you'll start to realize, "How can people not get this? How can people not see their experience that they're living through right now?"

You will be able to see what they're doing to themselves.

You will be able to see it in yourself and you will be able to see it in others.

That's what being an Expert Coach gives you access to.

Not only will you get access to that, but you'll be able to take other people through that too, and then build a super successful business off the back of it.

This will mean that you can access a huge element in life where you are truly fulfilled doing something you truly love.

Being an Expert Coach gives you access to the greatest skill in the world, which will pay you a dividend in every area of your life and truly set you free.

Through transforming your client, you will in turn transform yourself at a profound level that will impact your life deeper than anything else you have ever experienced.

I just want you to take a moment to reread that and jot that down...

"Through transforming your client, you will in turn transform yourself at a profound level that will impact your life deeper than anything else you have ever experienced."

I just want you to sink that in...

"Your life deeper than anything else you will have ever experienced..."

Action

Write down the purpose of coaching.

Chapter 2

YOUR EXPERT COACHING GOAL

The secret to being an Expert Coach is being able to guide your client into responsibility.

In responsibility, every action, anything they want from their life, becomes possible.

Life is ups and downs.

Winning in life is about getting through the downs.

There is no perfect life. There is no right or wrong. There is no right way to live. There's no wrong way to live.

The goal is to help your client achieve a life that works for them.

This is what life is...

That's life.

And that's your client's life.

And that's why they need you to stay on track.

Your clients will want to avoid responsibility because it's easier.

The truth is, their life will never work if they do not take responsibility for everything in their life.

You want to help them get to a place where they can take responsibility for what their life is and what their life isn't.

Help them get rid of any victim mentality or entitlement.

Once they get to that point, they will be empowered from a humbled unassuming place, which is the place that will give them the most power and drive.

Action

Write down your Expert Coaching goal.

Chapter 3

CAUSE AND EFFECT LANGUAGE

This is one of the fundamentals of being and Expert Coach.

This is an Aristotle philosophy:

Cause or Effect

You can only be on one side.

You can't be on both.

It's black and white.

You can't be happy and sad at the time. At the same time, you just can't be both. You're one or the other.

You're either happy or you're sad. That's it.

You can't be depressed at the same time and be grateful at the same time.

You're either one or the other.

You're either grateful or you're depressed.

You can't make progress and regress at the same time.

You either progress or you progress. It's up to you.

You can't be empowered and disempowered at the same time.

You're either empowerment or you're in disempowerment.

You can't be a victor and a victim at the same time. You're either a victor or you're a victim.

You either do the work or you don't do the work...

And it's freeing when you look at it like that.

Your role as an Expert Coach is to help guide your client to empowerment in every decision they make.

Notice when they are stuck in a fixed view in life, when they are at "effect", through their language, and help them bring awareness to their language pattern so they can form a new belief. You help them to a new action step.

Which side of the "Cause or Effect" equation would you like to be on?

Decisive or indecisive?

So your role as an Expert Coach is to help them see blind spots, help them retrain their language and help them create new habits that form those new behaviours.

When you retrain language, you retrain reality.

So as soon as you say, "I'm handling it", you start to live on causality.

You start to live in empowerment versus struggling.

As soon as you say, "I'm beginning to get it", you start to create empowerment versus saying, "I don't get it".

As soon as you say, "I'm curious", you start to become empowered versus saying, "I am stuck".

As soon as you say, "I'm grappling with this", you start to grapple with it rather than saying, "I can't do this".

Notice it's empowerment versus disempowerment.

And it starts with what your language.

The language describes your reality.

What you say creates your reality.

So the truth is, you live in "cause", which is progression or "effect" which is regression.

Action

Write down every day for 90 days, "I take responsibility for everything in my life."

You'll take responsibility and you'll start to find yourself in empowerment every single day.

Chapter 4

WHY BEING AN EXPERT COACH IS DIFFERENT

The coaching industry is filled with some very unpractical ways to help clients and it is filled with companies that have lost sight of what really is important.

The landscape in this industry is very different right now...

I learnt the really hard way, so you don't have to by reading this book.

I spent well over a hundred thousand on coaching courses and I refined this over 10 years with clients in real time, so I know the difference between what works and what doesn't work.

The problem is a lot of schools of therapy and coaching certifications don't actually talk to the problem.

I'm going to lay the foundations for you for you as an Expert Coach so you can easily apply them with your clients, without fear or whether you're doing the right thing and, most importantly, without using complicated structures that take too long.

Here's the overview.

Think of the problem as a table.

A table only exists because of the 4 legs (the 4 pillars) supporting it.

Without the 4 legs (the 4 pillars), the table collapses.

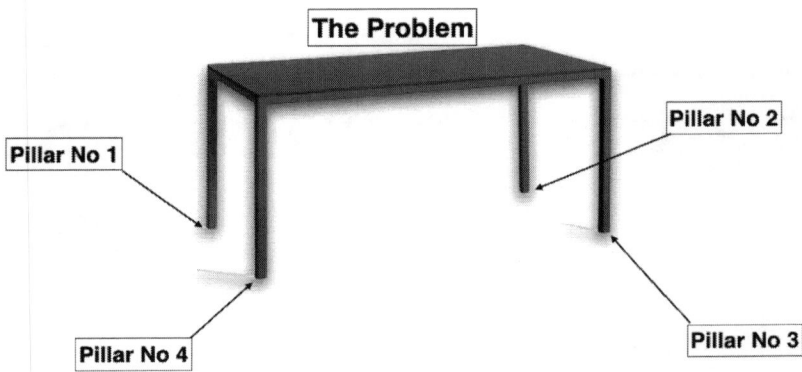

So the problem only exists because of the 4 pillars supporting it.

Therefore, we have to eradicate all four pillars for the problem to be collapsed.

The 4 Pillars are:

Pillar No 1: Diagnosis - How the reality of that problem was created

Pillar No 2: Breaking - How to break the belief that structures the problem

Pillar No 3: Retrain - How to retrain the behaviour so the problem doesn't recreate somewhere else

Pillar No 4: Compounding - Daily positive behaviours allowing new empowering behaviours to grow

That is the Expert Coach process.

Along the process and as you move through the pillars, you will have specific tools that you're going to use that will be covered in later chapters.

This is The Expert Coach Model.

We're going to diagnose the problem, then break the belief that structures the problem, then retrain the new behaviour so the problem doesn't come up elsewhere, and then compound on positive behaviours to allow new empowering behaviours to occur.

This will be a unique tool that you won't have used anywhere else, and it's super simple to use.

Action

Write out the 4 pillars that support the problem.

Chapter 5

WHY THE DEMAND FOR COACHING IS SO BIG RIGHT NOW

What are the facts in the market right now?

There is more free information available online than ever before.

This in turn, overwhelms the masses. And because this free information is unstructured and scattered all over the place, this means that demand for people wanting real help has gone up.

More free information is not the cure.

What your client needs is accountability.

They need structure.

What your client needs is you holding them to a higher standard.

What your client needs is you caring about them and standing for them more than they actually stand for themselves.

This is the main reason why the coaching market is growing so rapidly.

"But Ed, I see a lot of coaches who can't get clients."

It's true, there are a lot of coaches that can't market themselves to get clients.

This is not going to be a problem for Expert Coaches because in you becoming an expert you will be a problem focused coach.

If you get clear on the problem you solve and how you solve it, you will always get paid from this as a skillset.

But why is the demand for coaching so big?

The world population increases year on year.

Technology speeds up year on year.

Information exchange speeds up year on year.

And as a by-product, the world's problems get worse year on year.

You can see this in the stats.

Mental health year on year gets worse.

These are stats from the Mental Health Foundation, "It's estimated that one in six people now in the past week experienced a common mental health problem."

According to the charity Mind, "One in four people will experience a mental health problem of some kind. Each year, one in six people report experiencing a common mental health problem in any given week."

Obesity is also getting worse. The latest NHS figures revealed 20% of children are obese.

The number of adults who were overweight or obese in increased with age among both men and women. This was the highest among men aged between 55 and 64 where 82% of men were obese and women between 65 and 74 where 70% are now obese.

Divorce is getting worse.

Divorce is at the highest percentage increase in 50 years.

Data from the Office of National Statistics shows that divorces have risen by 18.4%.

Suicide is getting worse.

Death by suicide is skyrocketing, in young people in particular, and within males it's the most significant.

Unemployment is getting worse.

The UK unemployment rate has surged to some of its highest levels.

But here is the good news.

More people than ever are buying online.

Year on year online sales have gone up.

So here's more good news, people are craving for a holistic approach.

A high percentage now know that medication is not the cure to most problems.

The global e-learning industry has risen by over 135.9 billion alone, which means people are actually buying solutions to their problems.

People want to learn how to solve their problem.

Coaching is the cure.

The coaching industry is booming.

Tracy Sinclair, from the International Coaching Federation, states that "coaching is one of the fastest growing professions worldwide."

For this exact reason it works.

Coaching is the key to a fulfilled life.

Action

Write down why the demand for coaching presents an opportunity for you specifically.

Chapter 6

THE TOP COACHING FEARS AND HOW TO BUST THEM FAST

Most coaches fail to get results with clients based on their own belief system.

So we need to have a look at your own belief system so that we get the best results for you and your client.

You can't level up a client if your own belief system stops you from creating possibilities.

What this means for you in the future, as you look at your own belief system, is that you won't feel worried or out of your depth at any stage because it will become step-by-step for you. You will become an Expert Coach who can handle any situation and any problem.

The truth is, without these fears, you will accelerate your learning potential ten times faster.

Traditional coaching methods do not address these core fears of the coach themselves.

It's okay to be imperfect as you go through your coaching journey. The world is far too worried about trying to be perfect at everything.

I embrace and accept that I am so imperfect. I would even say that that's been one of my "secret sauces" to being able to be where I am today because I'm okay with being imperfect.

And so I'm going to let you be imperfect too.

As a coach, as in life, you are going to make mistakes and that's going to be okay. There's nothing wrong with making a mistake.

As Einstein says, "Those that have tried nothing new, have never made a mistake."

We have to make mistakes.

I am the most imperfect coach you've ever met. And that's why I'm excited to guide you through.

I've made more mistakes than I've had successes.

And so that's what's going to be exciting. You don't have to be perfect anymore. You don't have to fear anything!

But what are the top coaching fears?

I actually went out and researched this over a couple of years.

I went into coaching groups on Facebook, assessing, posting, seeing what people are talking about, talking to people at events, etc. and the number one coaching fear was *not being able to get results with clients*.

Even more interesting was that *making the client worse* was high up on that list.

So coaches were worried about actually making the client worse through their coaching.

Saying the wrong thing and not knowing what to say were high up on the list.

Not fully understanding the problem as the client sees the problem was on there too. This will be a big part of stage one of becoming an Expert Coach where you're going to learn how to diagnose the problem.

Others included:

Being out of their depth

Not knowing what value is for your client so they continue with you

Not knowing how to get clients who are willing to pay 2K plus for coaching

Not being able to get results with clients comes from the deepest human limitation of not being enough.

The other fears then stem from that.

No matter how successful people become, I have noticed that unless they do the work on *not being good enough* or *not being enough*, it still just keeps coming up.

The Expert Coach Model will eradicate this within you, and you will then be able to eradicate this within your clients too. And with that, when you are helping others and giving back to others, then in turn you start to grow at a whole different level.

And this is how to bust these fears fast.

Becoming an Expert Coach is designed around eradicating the biggest problems.

Complete the work and we'll get rid of any fears one by one.

What this means for you in the future is that you get access to the greatest skill in the world.

This will pay you a dividend in every area of your life.

It will set you free.

Expert Coaching is a high income skill so it can be used in many different ways, whether you have your own business or not, it doesn't matter.

Whether you work for a corporate or not, it doesn't matter.

If you're uplifting your skill set through this, you will become a high valued individual.

Without the skill of being an Expert Coach, growing a business is just not possible.

Without the skill of being an Expert Coach, having a successful relationship is not possible.

Without the skill of being an Expert Coach, having health is not possible.

So I want you to know this skill set that you're learning will impact your business, your career, your relationships with yourself and others, your health, and so much more.

Action

Write down which is your top fear so you know which one it is.

Rate it currently out of 10

1 is it's not a big fear

10 is it's a big fear

We are going to check up on it later and notice that score going down

Next, write down now what action do you need to commit to now to reduce that score.

Chapter 7

SO YOU KNOW YOU ARE IN SAFE HANDS

If we haven't met before, my name is Ed J C Smith and all I have ever done, all my life, is coach people.

I want to share with you how I started on my coaching journey.

I wasn't a high achiever growing up.

In fact, I failed badly at school.

It wasn't because I wasn't putting the effort in or because I was lazy, but it just didn't seem to really work.

It was like my brain just didn't seem to work like everyone else's. I was slower.

I thought differently and exams just didn't seem to go well.

And so, I wasn't some sort of hardcore learner, it wasn't easy for me.

I had to struggle to get to where I am today and so you get it much easier just by standing on my shoulders.

Growing up in my house was tough.

Even though we were defined as middle class and we lived in a nice area, I wasn't happy and I was very lost in life.

My father and I just didn't quite see eye to eye. He expected more from life and he worked night and day to achieve it — but he always felt short-changed.

We all felt his frustrations.

Our relationship was never good.

As the middle child in my family, somehow much of his anger was directed at me.

He was the exact opposite from me. He had a very fixed view of life and what I should do with mine.

One day we had a huge argument, and I ran out the house.

I found my way to a railway station where I stood on the edge of the platform and prepared to jump in front of the next train going through at high speed.

However, at the moment I was about to jump into the train, two hands on my shoulders ripped me back into safety.

And then he sat me down and he made me see a different view of life, he made me see a different path in life and he made me commit to a simple, simple belief that I still do today, a simple promise that I still make every single day.

I was given a second chance at life and that day I made a promise.

I made a promise that I still keep today...

...that promise to simply never give up on my dreams.

That turning point changed the entire course and direction of my life.

I was coached back to life by someone who didn't even know really what they did for me.

I believe life is just moments. And a simple moment can alter the entire path of your life.

I am sure that there are times that you too can recall a moment when it all transformed for you.

I hope that in turn, just by getting this book, that right now becomes a moment that it all transforms for you too.

I was coached back to life by someone else. So, in turn, I started on my coaching journey also and got addicted to helping other people.

I started as a one-to-one coach.

I started renting space in Wimpole Street in London and I started practicing sharing my skills.

I got some great coaching.

I fell in love with the process.

I started in the gym as a glorified cleaner and I just started practicing talking to people in the gym.

I moved into the health space initially, then into the depression space, and then into the relationship space and then into a corporate coaching consultancy.

I worked for over 12 years mastering transformation just to one-on-one before I started even going to large groups.

I started with my groups from a relatively short amount of time to getting more and more people turning up.

And all I was doing was practicing my coaching techniques.

I have lived this!

I don't feel like I'm any smarter than anyone else but when I talk to people who are struggling to break through, I am speaking from experiences I have had myself.

I built myself up from the scrawny, acne-scarred teenager who was about to end his life to becoming a successful business owner who has helped everyone from people with depression to others with relationship problems or corporate clients struggling to overcome their own limitations.

And, to give you the God's honest truth, the business stuff is all good. I've been doing that a long time...but I've been doing coaching a lot longer.

So, my actual core skill set is, coaching, that's what I spent my entire life doing.

The business was a by-product of building my own consultancy, and then people started coming up to me and saying, "Oh, can you help me do this?"

But, the core element of where the true strength comes, is this ability to coach.

Chapter 8

YOUR FIRST CLIENT AND ALL THAT COME AFTER THEM

Who is your first client?

Your first client is you!

So as you become an Expert Coach, I want you to know that you will also be getting access to a whole different area.

As I said earlier, you'll be getting access into the relationship that you really want to get.

You'll be getting into the health that you really want to get.

You'll be getting into the emotional well-being to a whole different level.

As you get stronger within yourself, you will self-generate the results you see in your clients.

You will also self-generate letting go of any limitations that have held you back up till now.

As you help and coach people, you will find your own internal limitations start to slip away.

As you help and coach people, you'll find your own possibilities start to grow.

This is the universal law of life.

You either grow or you die.

That's what the plant does too.

Plants either grow or die.

That's just fact, that's universal law.

The plant either does the work to grow or doesn't do the work and dies.

And so therefore you either progress or regress in life. And it's up to you.

You either do the work and progress, or you do not do the work and you die.

You can't get stuck in between, that's what is exciting.

There's no grey in this area, you either do the work or you don't do the work.

You can't do both.

You're either moving forward or moving backwards, it's up to you.

If you doubt your ability with a client, then refer them to someone else. If you doubt your ability to handle them or the problem at any stage, refer them out.

This is very powerful. This is not weak.

This sends a very strong message to your mind that you are in control. You make the decisions.

Confidence comes from competence.

The more you practice, the more effective you're going to become.

Just like a wall, it must be built up one brick at a time.

We all start from somewhere.

No one is born confident, be clear on who is your ideal client and who is not, is your power.

This will set you free.

This will allow you to build incredible strength.

Not everyone is open to you.

Not everyone will like you and not everyone deserves to sit at your table, and it's your choice, not theirs.

Action

Write down who your first client was.

Chapter 9

THE TRUTH OF LIFE

In life, your being either grows or dies.

In life, your health either grows or dies.

In life, your love either grows or dies.

In life, your business either grows or dies.

It's up to you.

In life, you either grow or die.

It's up to you.

So we can be at either regression or progression.

Regression: "You perceive yourself as stuck, but yet time goes on moving forward. This means you're not actually stuck, you're going backwards."

Progression: "1% improvements from the previous date."

This is what you're going to do for yourself, and this is also what you are going to do for your client.

So your goal with your client is to stop them from regressing.

Your goal with your client is to keep them progressing.

But how to move through?

With regression, we wait to feel good to do the work.

With progression, you do the work to feel good.

There's a distinct difference between regression and progression.

Regression is that you wait to feel good to do the work, and progression is that you do the work to feel good.

Your brain can only do one or the other.

For example, you can only cry or laugh. You can't do them both at the same time.

So you either regress and you don't do the work or you progress and you do do the work.

Action

Write down the truth of life.

Chapter 10

YOUR SACRED FOUR ACCOUNT

Fulfilment occurs when you consistently have built your being account, and when you have consistently built your energy account, and when you have consistently built your love account, and when you have consistently built your impact account.

1) Your being account.

This is your emotional wellbeing. You can design this for yourself but, in some shape or form, it's working on that emotional being. It could be mantras, meditation, journaling, ice baths, whatever you want to do.

2) Your energy account.

   Quite simply, what you put into your body and how you exercise on a daily basis.

3) Your love account.

   You must build your love account, your equity within that account, and simplistic ways to do it.

4) Your impact account.

   Whether you're making an impact in your career or your business.

You'll be scoring those points right now as to how fulfilled you are.

This is really important for you and for your client. And this is an ongoing process.

It never stops.

The only time it stops is when you die. Remember, you're either growing or dying.

This is a continued process of finding fulfilment in your life.

And this is measurable, and this is manageable and it's consistent on a daily basis.

This is going to be the same system that you use for your clients also.

So here are the sacred four definitions:

Being - your ability to be anxiety free, grateful, and present with your emotional wellbeing.

Energy - your ability to generate energy, be productive, stay focused and complete tasks.

Love - Your ability to generate love within your personal and professional life, including self-love and external love.

Impact - Your ability to generate a value in the world and generate an income in return.

So we are going to score each of your sacred four right now from 1-10, 10 being the highest:

Being	1	2	3	4	5	6	7	8	9	10
Energy	1	2	3	4	5	6	7	8	9	10
Love	1	2	3	4	5	6	7	8	9	10
Impact	1	2	3	4	5	6	7	8	9	10

We must measure our performance.

If you don't measure it, it can't then be improved.

If you don't measure it then it will become lost and you won't ever realize how far you've come.

You have to benchmark this.

You have a clear point structure to me to measure your performance daily.

I do this still every single day so I know when I've had a great day.

You now have a clear point structure to train your clients on too so that they can improve daily.

This is how you're going to hold your client accountable.

So, they're going to have to do action tasks.

You're going to pick a, a core area that they want to focus on.

Maybe they want to focus on their emotional wellbeing.

So we get that sorted first and then we can move on to the health.

And then we can move on to the love, and then we can move on to the impact.

Now, of course, at different stages, some will be driven more by the emotional wellbeing, some will be driven more by energy, some will be driven more by love, some will be driven more by impact.

The goal is to get all four accounts working well.

It's easier to start with one account first and then build up.

Again, assess your client. Notice if they are overwhelmed.

And this is an ongoing process. This never stops for the rest of your client's life or your life.

We all have to work on these accounts.

You have to work on your being account every single day, your energy account every single day, your love account every single day, and your impact account every single day.

There are no day is off.

This is your life.

This is what your life is made out of, and this is a fulfilled life.

All we need to do is work on these four accounts for the rest of your life, and you're going to have an amazing life.

And this is everything you need to really transform someone's life.

We're talking about fulfilment.

And when we're talking about fulfilment, the truth is, most people won't get access to what you are getting access to.

All you have to do is just repeat it and go through the process.

Action

Give yourself a score on your Sacred 4 every day for the next 90 days and see what you notice.

Chapter 11

WHY ALL THAT MATTERS IS YOUR CLIENT RESULTS

We live in a world that is very time poor.

And we live in a fast-paced information-sharing world.

People are overwhelmed.

People have very short attention spans, like goldfish, like three seconds.

The only thing that truly grabs their attention is if you solve a problem, a problem they have that is causing them pain now.

If they're not in pain with a problem that you're talking about, they're not your ideal client.

If there is no problem that they have, there is no value to share.

So, all that matters is your client results.

Because the truth is, the quicker your client experiences a result and the faster they begin a new belief system, the more likely they will continue with you and thus get continued tangible results, and benefit from your service.

Off the back of those results, it will be easier for you to grow your coaching business when it is focused on generating results for your clients.

Most coaching certifications completely miss out to design the coaching process to help you actually build your business at the same time as you get your client the results that they need and want.

So what is a coaching result?

A coaching result is helping your client perceive a new reality, a new view of life.

A coaching result is helping your client cultivate their answers that allow them a new possibility for themselves.

A coaching result is helping your client them get over their past and live life in the present.

Action

Write down what is the most important thing about coaching.

Chapter 12

WHAT IS TRANSFORMATION?

Transformation is a process by which one figure, expression, or function is converted into another one of value.

Words create a reality.

Reality creates a way of thinking, being, and acting.

Transformation occurs through language.

Transformation occurs through talking.

However, there is talking and there's coaching.

Coaching is very different to just talking.

Coaching takes your client through a journey of transformation, so it's structured language.

However, transformation occurs before you even speak based on what you believe is true.

So where do our beliefs come from?

Our beliefs come from seven key areas that condition beliefs:

- Environment
- Parents
- Education
- Social Groups
- Experiences

- Repetition
- Impact

We have to self-audit the working environment.

We have to question whether the beliefs are ours or our parent's.

We have to ask how our education has reinforced our past beliefs.

We have to assess how our social groups are impacting our beliefs.

We have to assess how our past bad experiences hold us back.

We have to look at how many time the belief has been repeated and the intensity of how the belief was delivered so we can assess the impact.

Now I'm sure you know that your conscious mind, the goal setter, is 5% of our brain. Your unconscious mind, the goal getter, is 95%.

So we're going to have to do the work in the unconscious mind.

Your unconscious mind is driven by what you believe to be true.

So if we work on the beliefs, then we can get that unconscious change.

You don't choose what you believe, you absorb them randomly like a sponge.

An empowering belief or a disempowering belief is formed based on six main points.

Here's what it looks like:

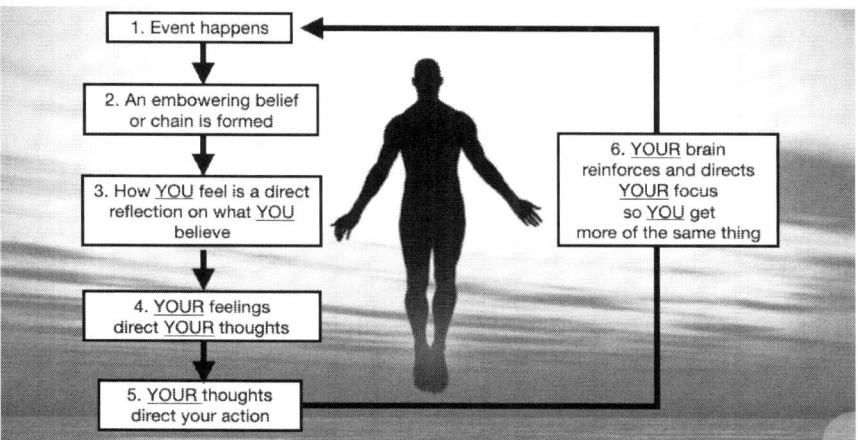

Have you ever noticed sometimes you've been on a roll, and good things happen, and then more good things happen, and you continue to have good things?

Have you noticed sometimes you've been on a roll the other way, where a bad thing happened, then another bad thing, and another bad thing?

That's how the thinking goes; it goes in patterns.

And so, we adopt these beliefs, and transformation occurs rapidly.

By adopting these sets of beliefs, your clients will transform in front of your eyes.

You will become someone that brings the spark, regardless of how you feel.

People will attract to you because of how you think.

People will ask you, "Can you bottle up that energy that you have?"

They are quite simply frameworks that allow new views to appear.

Sit with them.

Put them on like a jacket or a new skirt and take them for a trial run. They become more comfortable to wear when you wear them in a little.

Just like a new pair of shoes, they can be a little stiff at first. In time, they will feel just as comfy as your favourite slippers or your favourite jumper that you wear daily that makes you feel good.

Your results are tied to your belief potential.

As you grow, your ability to transform will grow too.

As your thinking expands, so do your client results.

I had a counsellor once, during a live event I was running, stand up triggered by something I'd said and shout at me, "Ed, but people can't change. People don't change."

I answered, "They don't if you hold that belief. That is true."

And so, your results are tied to your belief potential.

So, your client's beliefs can be retrained.

Your beliefs can be retrained every day, and it doesn't have to take years and years.

It can happen in a moment of a thought.

Action

Write out the seven key areas that condition beliefs.

Chapter 13

THE EXPERT COACH TRANSFORMATIONAL BELIEF SYSTEM

This is something you are going to practice both with yourself and with your clients so that it becomes second nature to you.

 Evaluate on behaviour. Don't judge the person; evaluate what behaviour is currently occurring.

 Xenium – to give respect. **Respect their view** and give respect to it, even if their view is different to your view or that of others.

 People have everything they need to achieve within them now. There is no such thing as an unresourceful person, just unresourceful states of being.

 Everyone is doing the best they can with the resources they have available.

R — **Resistance** is a sign of lack of rapport.

T — **The words we use** mean whatever we want them to mean.

C — Coach on the incompleteness. Complete on all areas.

O — **Only feedback**, there is no failure.

A — **Accept** people and problems as they are.

C — **Communication** is the response you get back.

H — **Honesty** is the cure for all.

Let's build these out even more.

E - Evaluate on behaviour

The most important information about a person is the behaviour they are currently adopting by the world in which they are being used.

If someone is angry at you, it doesn't mean they're an angry person.

It's just at that moment their behaviour is anger.

There's a difference between seeing someone as an angry person and knowing that they have an angry behaviour, because behaviours can be changed and transformed in seconds.

Similarly, just because someone has depression, it doesn't mean they have to have it for the rest of their life.

It means that they've been doing depression for a long time.

And so, therefore, behaviour can change rapidly.

X - Xenium means to give with respect.

Respect their view and give respect to it, even if their view is different to your view or that of others.

We can't judge.

We must not judge.

And as you coach more people, you start to be more open to more different people's perspectives and views in life.

P - People have everything they need to achieve within them now

There's no such thing as an un-resourceful people, just un-resourceful states of being.

People are not broken; they just have barriers to the ability to move forward.

And when you see someone as having that huge amount of resourcefulness, then no amount of people are unresourceful.

Every person is capable of achieving whatever they need to in life.

E - Everyone is doing the best they can with the resources they have available

Here is forgiveness for you...

You know, your parents were doing the best that they could with the resources they had available.

They didn't have the books that you now have today.

They didn't have this information.

You are instantly upgraded by reading this.

Your clients will be instantly upgraded by going through your service.

Everyone is doing the best they can with the resources they have available to them.

R - Resistance is a sign of lack of rapport

There are not resistant clients, just inflexible communicators to break through the resistance.

So, you have to build your communication skills and get better as a communicator.

T - The words we use mean whatever we want them to mean

We choose the meanings of words.

The words we use mean different meanings to different people, depending on their meanings.

And so, when we understand that words have different meanings to different people, then we can have different situations.

It reminds me of when I used to run a coaching program for a charity that helped homeless people.

I was presenting and this one particular guy got really upset with the situation and the process and if front of everyone he called me "a prick".

I smiled and replied, "Okay, that's cool."

And someone else then said, "Why aren't you offended from that?"

"Well, you know," I said, "I don't think that's such a bad thing. Me and my brother used to call each other "prick" when we were growing up and we used to laugh about it."

We can have very different associations to certain words.

Words mean different things to different people.

Someone was really offended because someone called me that, whereas I wasn't offended because I don't have that association or meaning to it.

We choose our meanings.

C - Coach on the incompleteness

Coach on where there is incompleteness; work on completing all areas.

Everyone can be whole and untriggerable.

Untriggerable is this concept that you can walk through life with inner peace, without worrying about the external factors.

You can't control the external factors; however, you can control your reaction to the externals, and that's because we become untriggerable.

So, we coach on completeness to get this.

O - Only feedback, there is no failure

It's just feedback.

It's just data that you can put back in so that you can become stronger.

A - Accept people and problems as they are

It's just the way it is.

Accept them with no judgement, no resistance, no attachment, and transform the behaviour.

C - Communication is the response you get back

What you put out comes right back to you.

H - Honesty is the cure of all

The truth will set you free.

The truth will set your clients free.

The truth opens up a new view of being for your client.

With the Expert Coach Transformational Belief System installed in your thinking, you will transform your client just by thinking and acting through this view of life.

You must write this out, and you must develop your own meanings to this.

Practice using it and start collecting stories that make sense to you.

It does take some time, but just go through it, and it'll start to make sense.

Every time you go through it and you get a new story, it will make more sense.

Action

Write out all 11 steps of The Expert Coach Transformational Belief System by hand.

Chapter 14

WHY STRUCTURE IS SO IMPORTANT

The truth is, you just can't scale results without structure.

And I've seen it time and time again.

When I say "scale", I'm talking about having hundreds and hundreds and hundreds of client results.

It's impossible to get that many results without following structure.

The structure allows you to scale.

It's very difficult to tangibly monitor and measure results without structure.

At times it feels like a bit like you're the Karate Kid. I get it.

But why did Mr. Miyagi have Daniel waxing on and waxing off?

Because when it's needed, because he did all the tasking, he was able to block the kicks and the punches.

And so Mr. Miyagi was teaching Daniel a system and a structure that allowed him to protect himself and get a result.

You need a structure that will protect you when you are coaching and you need a structure what will get the results that you want for your clients.

Without structures, you will not be able to protect yourself.

Without structures, you will not be able to get results.

Your emotional wellbeing is very, very important. It's a very important part of that process.

You will be talking about people's negative emotions and without the structure you are exposing yourself to that.

From the structure we can develop adaptability.

Bruce Lee said, "Empty your mind. Be formless. Be shapeless like water. Put water in a cup, become the cup. Put water in a teapot, become the teapot. Water can flow or creep or drip or crash. Be water, my friend."

A lot of people think this is "just be fluid" without structure.

But what Bruce Lee is saying is to become formless and shapeless. Be adaptable.

If there's a cup in front of you, the water adapts to the size of the cup.

If there's a teapot, the water adapts to the size of the teapot.

Now, here's the truth about this.

You must access a clear structure because Bruce Lee did structures for years, years and years.

That's what martial arts is. Martial arts is set structured movements.

Once you get the set structured movements in place, then you can be formless.

You must learn and understand the structure.

You then repeat that structure until the structure is mastered.

Then you access formless, shapeless, adaptability because the structure allows you to hold any shape that you choose.

When you have a solid session structure in place, you will be very clear.

Action

Write down why structure is so important.

Chapter 15

BECOME CERTAIN

At the end of the day, if you are clear, your clients will become clear.

Clarity is power, but more importantly, clarity is powerful.

Your clients are buying clarity.

Without the structures, you cannot be clear.

Without structure, your client will not trust you.

All you need is to be more certain than your client.

Your client is buying your certainty because they're uncertain about what they're going through.

Certainty comes from confidence.

Confidence comes from competence.

Through this process, we become competent. And we become competent by doing, not by thinking about doing.

There's a big difference.

Let me tell you about my first corporate client that took me on for a coaching role.

Senator Sergey, President of the Pic Group.

I'll be honest, I was way out of my depth.

Somehow I was able to secure the contract and it was way beyond me and my skillset at that time.

But I was just doing the best that I could with the resources I had.

Now, because of my certainty, he assumed I was more competent in the things that I was talking about than he was.

So he started giving me ownership of things within his company.

At first, I was specifically looking after just one area and I was just providing a consultancy service to him, specifically around his wellbeing.

This was an area that I really understood.

And because of my certainty here, I started integrating within his company as a sort of "second hand".

I started coming to meetings, listening in and giving feedback because he respected my ability to be confident and competent.

When I tell this story, people always ask, "Were you just hanging in there?"

I was. And I was learning on the go.

Learning on the go is the goal.

He started offering me tasks that were just crazy.

For example, we were dealing with relationships between his management team, and he said, "Ed, you talk a lot about relationships - the ship of relating."

And I said, "Well yeah, it's a core componence. Business is understanding relationship equity."

And he said, "Look, I like this concept about a ship. Let's build a boat."

"You find someone to build it and then teach us to sail it."

In that moment, I could say, "I don't know how to do that."

Or I can say, "I can handle anything, and I'll find out how to do that."

I chose the latter.

Now, I'm not saying we ended up winning The America's Cup, because we didn't.

But that wasn't the goal.

The goal was to do these trainings on the boat, learn how to sail, and build better relationships with the managers in the process.

I'd never sailed a boat.

I'd never even sailed a topper.

But we started renting out boats for the weekend so we could get a feel for it.

And then I found some America's Cup coaches and sailors, you know, people to actually teach me how to operate one.

And that's what I did.

Four years in a row we went to the British Virgin Islands to sail, building up the team, and having a world class experience.

I couldn't imagine that I'd ever end up doing something like this.

The truth is, I took a two-week training course with the America's Cup sailors and I broke down the systems and the structures so I could understand it.

And then I got them over to help us implement that, while I ran the relationship training.

What I want you to get from this is that you can do anything when you start to become more resourceful.

I got three E's at school and now I was teaching someone how to sail a boat having never sailed one myself, having only just learnt how to do it and never having been on water in a boat!

You just have to be more certain than your client. That's it.

I was just rocking up saying, "We've got this."

Now, if I hadn't have said that, then I would've lost my position within the Pic Group. And I would never have maintained that client as long as I did.

And so you can immediately level up your game.

And so sometimes people say, "Well, is that authentic?"

To which I say, "I was saying that I am going to handle it."

And I did handle it.

That's what I'm saying.

I'm not saying this is a "fake it 'till you make it".

This is not.

There's nothing fake about it.

You're saying, "I can handle it."

There's a difference.

I didn't say that I had it all sorted or that I'd done it hundreds of times.

That's not the truth.

The truth is, I'm going to sort this out. We're going to handle it and we're going to rock it out.

Just be more certain and you're going to be okay.

You can't be in the race of life unless you start and stay committed.

Life is a race to the end.

Just enjoy that race and enjoy the process and just be in the game.

That's the whole thing.

Just be in the game of life.

And it doesn't matter how fast you go, it's that you never stop.

Action

Write down why certainty is so important.

Chapter 16

HOW TO APPLY THE SOLID SESSION STRUCTURE

The purpose of every session you have with your client is quite simply to get them from where they are now, to closer to where they want to be in every single session.

They should be progressing further forward every single session.

That's it.

That's the goal.

A	B
Where They Are Now	Closer To Where They Want To Be

Here's the 7-point Solid Session Structure to get them from Point A to Point B every single time:

1) Expectation

You need to set the expectation at the beginning.

You're simply setting the expectation of each session. Say what is actually going to happen.

And sometimes at the beginning those expectations may be a little bit softer, but as you do this more you can adapt this as you want.

2) Tasking

Next you're going to set and talk about the tasking, right at the beginning.

Because there has to be some sort of action and implementation done on their part.

So if it's the first session, you say, "Look, we're going to do some tasking."

And if it's a follow up session you're checking on the previous tasking here, so did they do the tasking from the last session. And if not, why not?

3) Diagnose

Then you're going to diagnose the problem as they see that reality. So, uncovering the limiting belief so we can break that.

4) Break

Then you're going to break that belief about that problem, breaking the hold of that limiting belief.

5) Retrain

Then you're going to retrain that belief so it doesn't come up again.

6) Compound

Then you're going to compound on that and hold them accountable.

7) Remind

And then you're going to remind them to do some tasking.

That's how the session goes and that's the structure you're going to use every time.

You're setting the expectation.

You're checking the tasking.

You're diagnosing the problem.

You're breaking the belief.

You're retraining that belief.

You're compounding on that.

And then you're reminding them to do the tasking.

Every single session, you're going to take them from where they are now, to closer to where they want to be.

And it's as simple as that.

And what this means for you moving forward is that you have a clear structure that works, which you can build on top of.

If you have a clear structure that your clients will trust, you will create your client results.

And results are all that matters.

Action

Write out the 7-point Solid Session Structure.

Chapter 17

UNDERSTANDING THE PROBLEM

Most coaches are not clear on how to diagnose the problem effectively.

Most coaches are not clear on how to break the belief that structures the problem.

And most coaches are not clear on how to retrain the behaviour so the problem doesn't recreate somewhere else.

Most coaches are not clear on how to compound on daily positive behaviours, allowing new empowering behaviours to grow, thus holding them accountable.

Remember, the problem is like a table.

The table only exists because of the 4 legs (the 4 pillars) supporting it. Without the 4 legs (the 4 pillars), the table collapses.

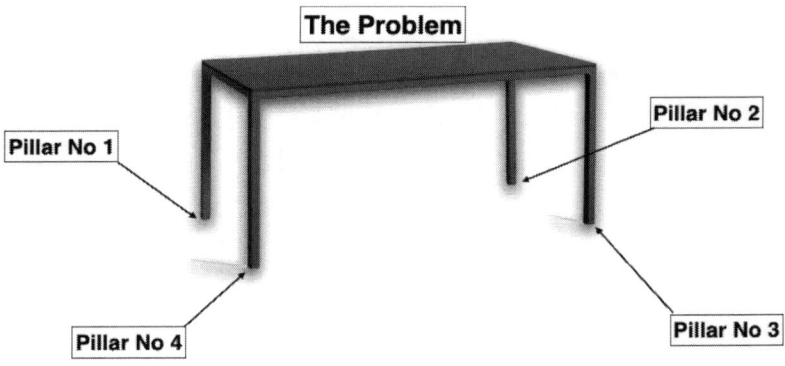

So the problem only exists because of the 4 pillars supporting it.

Therefore, we have to eradicate all four pillars for the problem to be collapsed.

The 4 Pillars are:

Pillar No 1: Diagnosis - How the reality of that problem was created

Pillar No 2: Breaking - How to break the belief that structures the problem

Pillar No 3: Retrain - How to retrain the behaviour so the problem doesn't recreate somewhere else

Pillar No 4: Compounding - Daily positive behaviours allowing new empowering behaviours to grow

That is The Expert Coach Process.

Remember, The Expert Coach Model looks like this:

We're going to diagnose the problem, then break the belief that structures the problem, then retrain the new behaviour so the problem doesn't come up elsewhere, and then compound on positive behaviours to allow new empowering behaviours to occur.

The model fits together in a beautiful system that keeps on growing your client.

But if we do not diagnose effectively, then a new problem occurs because the core belief is still held there that created the problem in the first place.

Then what happens is that negative belief builds, and frustration occurs.

The problem then strengthens and the disempowering emotion builds, and the whole thing just starts to create regression and the client continues to get worse.

Using The Expert Coach Model, we diagnose and so understand how the belief structures the problem.

Then we break the core belief that created the problem.

Then we retrain the new belief so it doesn't regress.

And then we compound that new habit, that new behaviour, so that we can get progression on a daily basis.

Action

Write out The Expert Coach Model.

DIAGNOSIS

Chapter 18

HOW THE REALITY OF THAT PROBLEM WAS CREATED

Our reality is created by three core concepts.

The brain can only process a very limited amount of information at one time.

Thus, the brain deletes, distorts and generalizes information to create an internal representation, a picture of that moment, and a view of that moment.

This picture is not a crystal-clear Instagram type picture. It's more of a hologram image of what's happening in that moment.

Thus, the brain creates a fixed view of reality directly linked to the current level of awareness that has been achieved and it links it to that picture.

That picture is made up of data, which is visual, auditory, kinaesthetic, and logic.

The thought is created by the internal representation, which directly affects the emotional state or feelings.

Emotional state or feelings directly affects our behaviour.

Our behaviour directly affects our ability to take action and then reinforces our thinking and reconditions our thoughts.

In its simplest form, an event happens and then a reality is formed.

So something happens and then our brain computes it and a reality is formed.

When the something happens, we go through a three-step process.

First, we think about it and have thoughts, creating an internal representation.

This creates an emotion, and we have feelings and create meanings to what has happened.

And then our behaviours are dictated by those feelings and meanings, and we take action accordingly and put language to it.

And these keep on reprocessing.

So when something happens or when we say something, that then creates a thought.

That thought stimulates the emotional state into the feelings and meanings, which then dictates the behaviours and actions and language.

So it's a Thought Cycle:

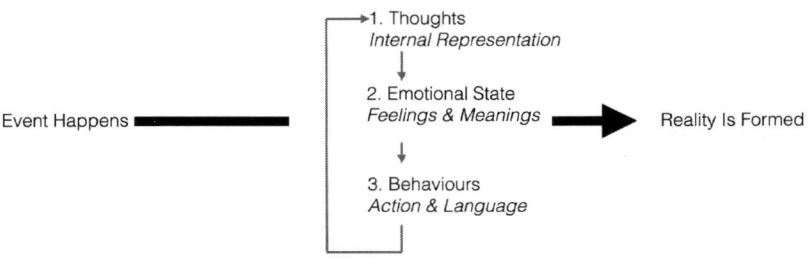

And so if we have a negative thought, then we have a negative feeling at stage two, then we have negative language that we use.

And then we start having more negative thoughts.

But if we start breaking what we say, for example if at step three we start changing our language, then we change our language which creates a different thought at step one.

When we create a different thought, we create a different emotional state. And when we create a different emotional state, then we create a different behaviour.

So if we change our language, for example "I'm handling it" versus "I'm stuck", the language of "I'm handling it" creates a different thought, which creates a different emotional state, thus creates a different behaviour.

And so these cycles can be broken by a range of different things, and they can be broken at steps one, two, or three. It doesn't matter. They're all intimately linked.

An event happens, it goes through this process of creating thoughts, emotional states and behaviours, and then a reality is formed.

The brain supports a pattern.

And this is why fixed views occur, because they keep on cycling the same thing.

So this is why your clients get stuck in certain thoughts, certain views, and it's our duty to help them out of that.

The thoughts create an internal representation in the brain, which creates an emotional state, feelings and meanings, which allows us to have a certain action and language.

And then this goes over and over and over again.

And our brain supports it, and this is why we get fixed patterns occurring.

And we create a reality through the language that we use gaging our experience.

The key is to look at the language, then look back to the behaviour, then look back to the emotional state and then the thoughts.

Language creates a reality, and reality creates a way of thinking, being, and acting.

So transformation occurs through language.

Transformation occurs through talking.

However, there is talking and there's coaching.

Coaching is very different to just talking.

Coaching takes your client through a journey of transformation, so it's structured language.

When we stop certain language, we stop certain thoughts, we stop certain emotional meanings.

And it all comes from understanding this three-step process.

Action

Write out the Thought Cycle.

Chapter 19

CREATING REALITY

Your reality is created by what you focus on.

The meanings you give to things and therefore the action you take because of it are all created by what you choose to focus on.

It never stops.

It's always operating within you and ultimately it will define what sort of reality you create.

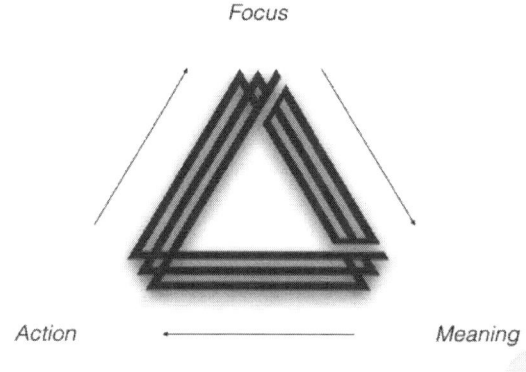

Your reality is defined by what you focus on.

Every day you have an opportunity to focus on all the good things in your life versus all the bad things that have happened in the past.

For the most part, you are completely unaware of your current trained focus.

If you focus on the good things then more good things will come to you, if you focus on the bad things then more bad things will start to happen.

What's wrong in life is always easy to notice however, what's right is equally easy when you train yourself to notice it.

Focus → Meaning → Action = Your Reality

Remember, your default settings have been influenced by the 7 factors:

- Environment
- Parents
- Education
- Social Groups
- Experiences
- Repetition
- Impact

These ultimately define your response to every situation you encounter.

Whether you find an empowering focus and label the experience with a powerful meaning that serves, strengthens and helps you move forward or the complete opposite, which is limiting and disempowering, is all down to what you focus on.

Let's take a simple phrase someone might say to you - "You should get a better job"...

Focus on the negative:

When considering that statement from a negative point of view, you may feel that it reflects directly on you.

For instance, you may feel that your efforts and therefore you, aren't good enough.

Or you'll feel maybe that your job is unattractive and therefore you are unattractive.

It may even be as simple as you believing that your friend is better than you, that you are lazy and you should do better.

Nonetheless, by seeing the phrase as a disempowering phrase, you are likely to be resentful towards your friend, resentful to taking positive action, as well as to your friendship in general.

Focus on the positive:

When considering the statement from a positive point of view, you may feel a sense of pride, that you are too good for your job, that you should be appreciated more, that you are better than what you are currently doing because you have so much potential.

Not only does hearing this make you feel so much better about yourself, but you hold your friend in higher regard as well.

That's a good friend who obviously cares enough to say something to you because they want to see you progress and help you move forward.

By labelling the experience as a good experience, you take positive action towards getting that better job and your friendship grows deeper and stronger.

Notice how these two scenarios create very different paths in your life.

If you focus on the negative, then you end up in a very different situation than if you focus on the positive.

That was one simple phrase.

Imagine all the times you've been unaware of focusing on the positive.

The problem here is that a lot of people walk around with the mask of positivity on when underneath they've been trained to focus on all the bad things happening around them.

People in the UK in particular are renowned for being negative and walking around pretending that everything is ok when it's clearly not.

I encourage you to take this simple example and look at it on a deeper level.

If you want more results in your life, it's time to question yourself.

Do you focus on the good things happening to you and do you really find the good in all the challenges that are sent your way? Or do you focus on the bad?

It's only under stress that you find out what someone's habitual hard wiring is.

We can all focus on the good, when everything in our lives is going well, we've food on our table and we're feeling really good.

What's it like when you are under stress?

That is the key barometer, that is the difference as to whether you'll be hugely successful or not. If you can't find the good when you're facing the bad times in your life, then you'll give up and stop moving forward.

An inspirational example is the story of Nelson Mandela. On being released from prison, he was asked, "what was it like being enslaved?"

He replied, "I wasn't enslaved, it was my choice to stay there. I was getting prepared for my mission."

He instantly changed the meaning of the statement by changing the focus.

He changed the focus from being 'enslaved' to 'getting prepared', which is so powerful.

This allowed him to continue getting stronger whilst he was in prison because, every year, he was given a choice to walk free only if he gave up his mission and went back to how it was before.

He refused and therefore changed the meaning of the statement.

If he hadn't done that, then he would never have made the 27 years of positive personal improvement and would've given up his mission.

Become more aware of what you're focusing on, the good things in your life versus the bad things and especially when you're stressed.

Your life is quite simple.

What you Focus on, what Meaning you choose to give it, is what Action you take from it.

What You Focus On You Get

*Action Is
Created In Language*

*What Meanings
You Choose*

And this goes round and round and round: what we focus on is what you get, what meanings you choose because of that action is created in language.

Your world is shaped by language.

Everything can be transformed because it's only how it occurs to you through language.

Through language your distinctions about life occur

Transforming the way the world occurs to you through your language is the most powerful way to transform your behavior and therefore your actions.

Action

What reality are you creating?

Write down what you focus on.

Then write down what meaning you are giving to what you focus on and what actions you are taking.

Chapter 20

EMPOWERING OR DISEMPOWERING

For every event that happens, you can either focus on it being empowering or disempowering.

You can do one or the other.

And your duty is to train your client to see empowerment, not disempowerment.

The meaning that we choose from that experience is our choice based on our current conditioning.

Then the action is a direct relation correlation to the meaning that we've given it.

So an event happens, for example you're pushed past your comfort zone, and you could either focus on disempowering versus empowering.

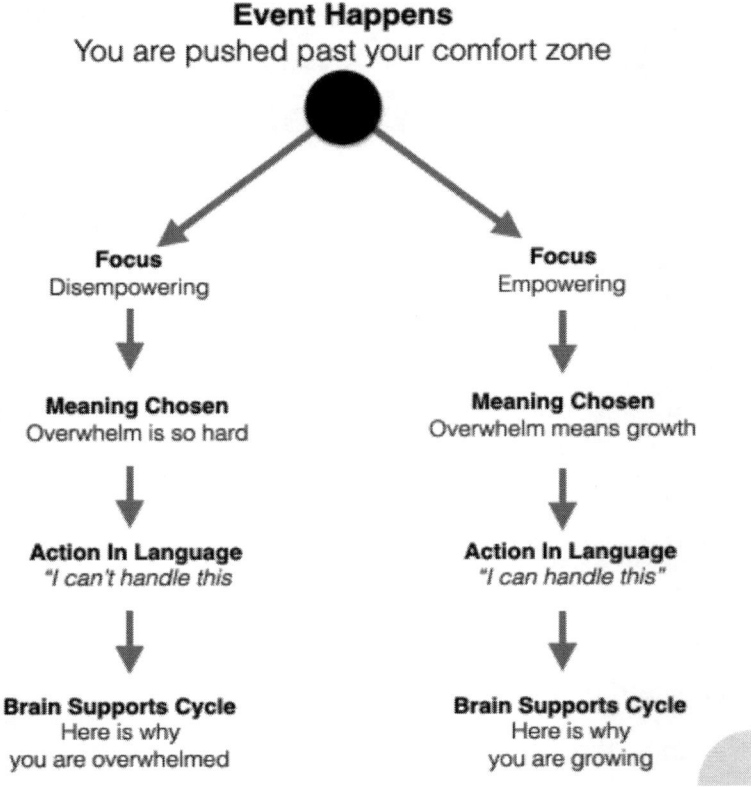

Event Happens
You are pushed past your comfort zone

Focus
Disempowering

Focus
Empowering

Meaning Chosen
Overwhelm is so hard

Meaning Chosen
Overwhelm means growth

Action In Language
"I can't handle this

Action In Language
"I can handle this"

Brain Supports Cycle
Here is why
you are overwhelmed

Brain Supports Cycle
Here is why
you are growing

If you focus on empowering, you get meanings: overwhelm means "growth" instead of overwhelm meaning "it is so hard".

Meanings on both sides of that create a certain belief and we take an action in language.

"I can't handle this" versus "I can handle this".

These are different realities.

These are not different words, these are different worlds.

And so when you can help your client see that through language they can create a different world, they can open up a whole different reality and a new landscape opens up for them.

Thus, the brain supports it.

If you language it as "you can't handle it", then the brain with support that with reasons why you are overwhelmed.

If you language it as "you can handle it", the brain will support you with why you are growing.

And therefore our goal is to continually help our client be unempowered versus disempowered.

Here are the two possible routes to someone texting you that they are going to be late:

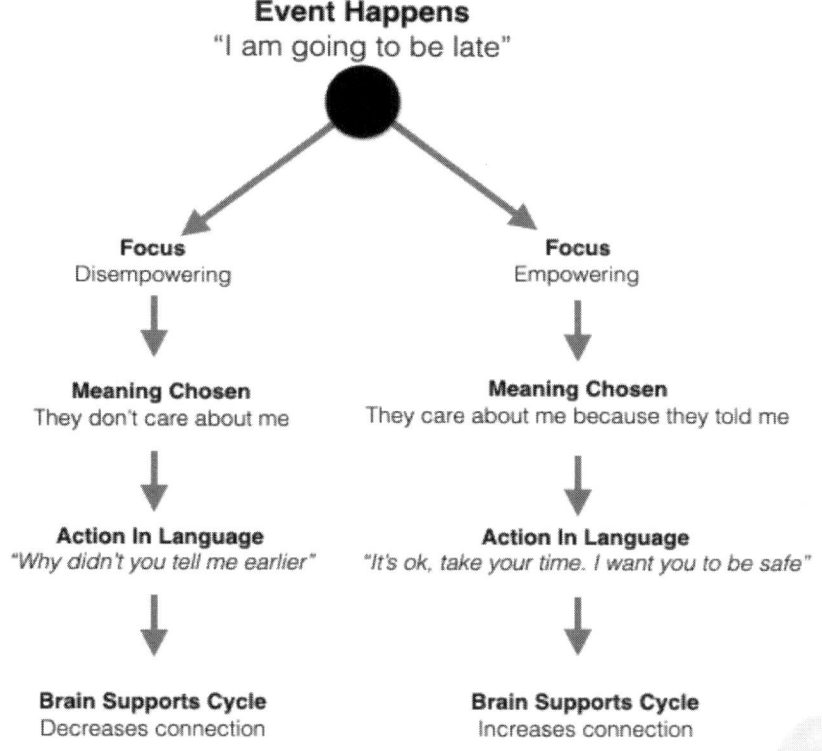

When you receive a text from someone and they say, "I'm going to be late", you can either focus on the disempowering or the empowering.

You could choose the disempowering meaning of them being late to be that, "They don't care about me".

Or you could choose the empowering meaning that because they told you it means "they do care about me".

Those are two different realities.

The reason that they sent you that text is because they actually care about you enough to say, "I'm going to be late".

These are different worlds.

You could have an argument off the back of it, "Why didn't you tell me earlier?"

Or you could take the empowering route.

These are simplistic things, but usually it's the small things that matter.

I've had it many times where a client has said that they almost crashed their car because they're rushing because they were so worried about their partner giving them a hard time for being late.

The brain supports the cycle and increases the connection.

Notice that if you go down the right-hand side of diagrams, you'll get an increased connection because there's a warmth and a care to that.

We've all been late for situations, that's what happens. It is what it is.

Sometimes you do the best you can and then things come in the way.

I remember driving to meet a client of mine and feeling really stressed trying to get across central London traffic.

And then he sent me a text saying, "I know you're probably a bit caught up. Don't worry. Don't rush. I don't want you to get a ticket or anything like that. I've blocked out the time. When you get here it's going to be great."

It literally just alleviated the whole stress of the situation.

It increases your connection versus the other way around.

If you have an argument, you decrease connection.

So you either increase connection or decrease it. That's it. It's as simple as that.

Your focus is either empowering or disempowering.

This applies to any task you undertake.

It might be a hard task.

It might be a task that you've never done before.

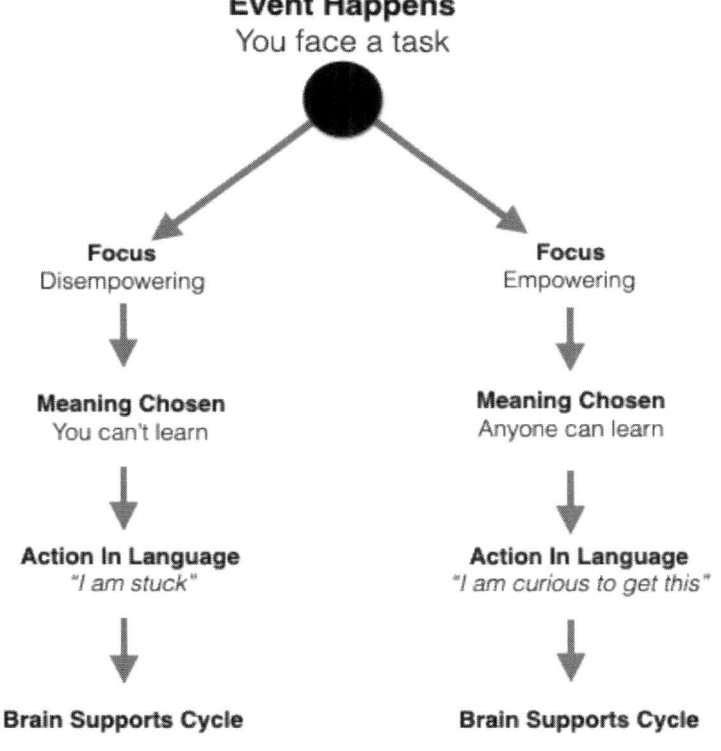

If you choose to give this task the empowered meaning that "anyone can learn" versus "you can't learn, notice that the language is very different.

I've got 71-year-old client that can put up ads on Facebook, yet I see people online going, "It's so hard. I'm stuck."

There are multiple ways in which we can get through anything we do depending on the meaning we choose and the language we use.

Again, the brain supports the cycle in both ways.

The language of "I'm stuck" will give you more of continuing to get stuck.

The brain will continue to support "I'm curious to get this" and keep you in empowerment.

So the question is, what keeps people stuck in these views?

It's a lack of awareness: a lack of an ability to see what is missing right now.

Thus they focus, thus focus them on what is missing right now to completion.

Your role as a coach is to help the focus on what is missing right now to completion.

Without coaching they will be in a blind spot, which is a story of the trust as they see it.

This keeps them fixed in a set view of life.

Action

Write down what disempowering language you have been using and what empowering language could you choose instead?

Chapter 21

BREAKING THE FALSE REALITY

There are 2 things at play here –

1) There's the story of what people say, and
2) There's a reality of what is actually (fact) happening

But the client is merging them...

You have to separate them so that there's a reality of what happened. Help them see what is the fact.

There are no feelings attached to that.

The feelings come in the story.

So we have to separate these two for the client so they are not thinking that the story is actually what happened.

And what happened is very different to the story.

There are facts and then there are meanings on those facts.

And so that's what we need to look at with our client so they can separate from what happened to a story and the meanings they're creating.

"Meanings"

Meanings define the experience of life.

Meanings are your client's story of what they believe is true.

People are naturally inauthentic about how authentic they actually are.

People lie about the fact that they lie.

It's not that they're bad people, it's just they are living in delusions of blind spots.

There's nothing wrong with that. It's not to judge it.

Our goal is to bring awareness around those inauthentic ways and help them be more authentic.

When I say "inauthentic", it's not from judgment.

What I'm saying is, people say, "I want to go to the gym", and then they don't do it.

People say they want to create a meaningful relationship and then they don't go and actually find someone.

People say they're going to call someone and then they don't do it.

These are all inauthentic.

It's not judging that. It's helping people become true to themselves.

When they say, "I'm going to do the work", they either do the work or they don't do the work.

Don't be that person that says that you're going to do it and then don't do it.

People are unconscious to being people.

People naturally want to be safe at all times, and that's why they have these stories.

People's safety is driven by what is easiest and most comfortable. Thus they create zones of comfort in which they exist.

The comfort zone, the story of limitation, is created in language.

Reality is created in language; possibility or impossibility.

Empowerment versus disempowerment is created in language.

Life is in language.

Declarations are made in language declaration.

When you say, "I'm going to marry you", it's done in language. So therefore, it's not true. It's not set in stone until they actually say, "I do".

When they say, "I do", then you're committed.

Nothing is true until it is in language.

Thought is not true until it is said.

Language dictates our experience: Lan-"gauge", the gauge which measures your experience in life.

Understanding Yourself

As Einstein says, "The significant problems we face cannot be solved at the same level of thinking we were at when we created them".

The goal of life is to become aware of ourselves so we can be fulfilled.

We do this by noticing when we are in a fixed view of life and find a new empowering meaning.

So it's truly understanding who you are; understanding yourself.

When you can do this, it's easier to help others do the same.

To understand yourself, you have to look what we know and what we don't know.

This concept prompted psychologists Joseph Luft and Harrington Ingram in 1955 to create The Johari Window:

	Known to self	Not known to self
Known to others	Arena	Blind Spot
Not Known to Others	Façade	Unknown

We know what we know, and others know it too (Arena) – Example: we know that the sky is blue

We don't know what we don't know (Unknown) – Example: we don't know what it's like to walk on Mars

We know what we know and what others don't (Facade) – Example: I know how to swim but my best friend doesn't

As a whole, people know what they know, and they know what they don't know.

For example, if you've never driven a car then you know that you don't know how to do that.

If you've passed your driving test, then you know that you know how to drive.

When it comes to being an Expert Coach, you will be able to see what your client knows they know and what they know they don't know.

And then there's the Blind Spot – what others know but we don't!

And this is where you come in as an Expert Coach.

And as part of being an Expert Coach, you need to be filling your cup first and increasing your awareness so there are no unknowns.

It's the unknown unknowns that we have to be open to uncovering for ourselves and then help our clients uncover.

And that's what awareness is.

Some call it enlightenment.

Ultimately, it's being someone that is free of stress, free of suffering, and that's fully aware of their negative emotions, how the triggers are formed, and knowing how to release them.

By embodying the Expert Coach methodology you can get to that stage where full awareness is possible for you and your clients.

Action

What reality are you creating?

Write down what challenge you are focused on right now that you could give a new empowered meaning to and thus take new action going forward.

Chapter 22

DIAGNOSING BLIND SPOTS

People live in blind spots.

When driving a car, if you've ever been hit or have hit something that was in a blind spot in your mirrors, you'll know that it literally comes out of nowhere.

And so that's what coaching really does, it brings awareness to the client's blind spot out of nowhere.

So how do we diagnose the blind spot the client is in?

We simply listen to our client and ask questions around their problem.

That's all we do.

We simply write down the key statements that they say, and we evaluate and inquire on those statements.

We are looking to separate the story versus what has actually happened.

So we're going to be looking at what they focus on, because what they focus on is what they get.

We're going to be looking at what meanings they have chosen, and what the action is created in language.

What You Focus On You Get

*Action Is
Created In Language*   *What Meanings
You Choose*

We must write our client's statements down.

So, what they're focusing on, what meanings are they choosing, and what are the language statements they use?

Just listen to the statements that they are saying and write then down.

You must, must, must write down the statements as you hear them in real time.

You listen to those statements as you hear them, and then you inquire on those statements.

From those statements alone, we can evaluate how they create that reality.

And you can read those statements back to them and hold them to those statements.

They must be held to the statements so that they get an understanding of the language they're creating.

Once they get an understanding of the language they're creating, then we can start to transform their reality.

We access their reality through their statements, and as we question the statements we'll uncover the beliefs, which sets us up to break them.

All you need to do is listen and write down their statements.

Then we can work on those statements, because it's those statements then define their reality, and we can understand how that reality is formed through those statements so that we can transform the belief that holds that reality in place.

Listen for how their language creates the reality.

Notice if that reality serves them or not.

If it serves them, even if it doesn't fit with your reality, then there's nothing you need to do to that.

Notice how that reality uses them.

When I say, "uses them", I mean like being used by a behaviour.

When someone's being angry, they're being used by anger.

When someone is depressed, they're being used by depression.

When someone's being frustrated or sad, they're being used by frustration or sadness.

Ask them questions that allow them to see a new view.

Ask them questions so they can create that new view for themselves. That's the key, so that they can create that for themselves.

You have to plant those seeds, so it actually cultivates inside of them.

If it doesn't cultivate from their view, then it won't stick.

When you take their statements and plant the seeds with your questions, then it starts to build a whole new way of thinking, and it will set them free.

The important part of coaching is to look at the statements and look for different points of view so we change the context of the statement.

When we change what the statement means we can create a new reality.

BELIEF BREAKING

Chapter 23

THE FOUNDATIONS OF BELIEF BREAKING

Having Diagnosed how the reality of the problem was create, we must now Break the belief that structures the problem, which is Pillar 2.

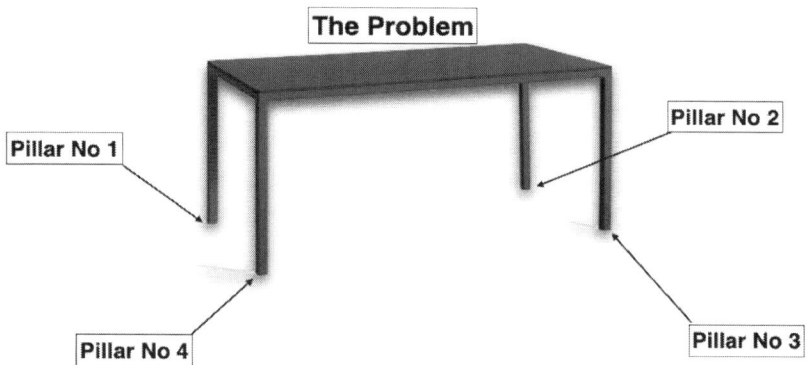

Remember the core beliefs, that are disempowering or empowering, will come from seven key areas:

- Environment
- Parents
- Education
- Social Groups
- Experiences
- Repetition
- Impact

An Expert Coach must discover which of them are empowering versus disempowering.

The environment conditions beliefs, so we can audit the environment in which the belief is working.

Parents condition beliefs, so we can question whether their parent's beliefs are theirs.

Education conditions beliefs, so we can see educational experiences are reinforcing past beliefs.

Social groups condition beliefs, so we can question the beliefs of their social peer groups.

Experiences condition beliefs, so we can look at how past experiences are holding them back.

Repetition conditions beliefs, so we can delve into how many times the belief has been repeated.

Impact conditions beliefs, so we can look at the intensity of how the belief was delivered.

Development Psychology

Gestalt therapy tried to fix the development stages until deeper examination brought up the readiness potential.

What that means, in essence, is that ages one to seven is your imprint period.

This is where you are picking up your emotions and your experiences from everything that's going on.

Between the ages of one and seven you're like a sponge; you just absorb what's happening around you.

Ages seven to fourteen are when your behaviours start to really kick.

This is your modelling period where you're looking at the behaviours of your parents.

Fourteen to twenty-one is the socialization period.

And twenty-one to thirty-five is the career period.

Imprint	Modelling	Socialisation	Career
1 - 7	7 - 14	14 - 21	21 - 35

Just so you know, your brain can keep on developing every step of the way. So don't think that past thirty-five, that that's it for your brain.

Neuroplasticity means that you can actually keep on training your brain every single day and your brain has no limitation in terms of its ability to learn.

In fact, the more you learn, the better your brain becomes.

As you go through these age stages, you pick up different beliefs. And of course, beyond thirty-five you can still continue to develop new beliefs.

Your beliefs structure your view.

Henry Ford said, "Whether you believe you can or you can't, then you're right."

This is one of the most famous constructs around what beliefs are.

What you believe becomes true.

Whether you believe that you can or you can't, you're right.

What you give energy to grows, so the more you start to see good stuff that will grow. The more you start to see bad stuff that will grow too.

This is a key Stoic exercise. Our perception is everything.

The ancient Roman philosopher Seneca said, "We dye events with our own colour."

We decide how we are going to look at it.

We decide the perspective we are going to bring to it.

We control the attitude, the approach, and the energy we bring to those situations. And that will make you much more successful in those situations.

There's a parable from 2,000 years ago that portrays this beautifully.

A Chinese farmer gets a horse, which soon runs away.

A neighbour says, "That's bad news."

The farmer replies, "Good news, bad news, who can say?" The horse comes back and brings another horse with him.

Good news, you might say.

The farmer gives the second horse to his son, who rides it, then is thrown and badly breaks his leg.

"So sorry for your bad news," says the concerned neighbour.

"Good news, bad news, who can say?" the farmer replies.

In a week or so, the emperor's men come and take every able-bodied young man to fight in a war.

The farmer's son is spared.

Good news, of course.

His neighbours said, "You're so lucky that you were able to keep your son at home, we had to part with ours. This must be the best day of your life?"

He replied, "Maybe."

It's easy to understand why the ancient story of the Chinese farmer resonates now, in times that seem way too full of bad news.

The tale of the farmer is said to be Taoist.

Taoist theology emphasizes themes such as naturalness, peace, effortless action, detachment and receptiveness.

The farmer's tale captures many of those.

In short, it reminds people that it's best not to get too upset or attached to what happens to us.

Even something that seems dark and confounding can turn out to be an opportunity, when looked on in hindsight.

Chapter 24

BELIEF TRANSFERENCE

Roger Banister broke the four-minute mile on 6th May 1954.

Now the truth is, before this happened, it was believed that it was absolutely impossible.

The science stated it was impossible.

Yet he did it.

He did the research, did the processes, and he broke that belief.

Because he broke that belief, forty-six days later, John Landy did the same thing.

This is belief transference.

Beliefs through stories, through talking, can transfer beliefs like a click of your fingers.

Another example of this is what is regarded as the biggest upset in boxing history; the 1990 heavyweight fight between Mike Tyson and Buster Douglas.

Going into the fight, Mike Tyson was the undefeated and undisputed heavyweight champion of the world and was very popular at the time.

Most considered this fight to be a warm-up bout for Tyson before meeting up with then-undefeated number one heavyweight contender Evander Holyfield.

Douglas was ranked as the number seven heavyweight by *Ring Magazine*, and had met with mixed success in his professional boxing career up to that point.

HBO boxing analysts expected to see "another 90-second annihilation."

From the beginning of the fight though, it was apparent that Douglas was not afraid.

Early on, Douglas was more agile than Tyson and out landed Tyson in exchanges.

Douglas would still dominate the middle rounds, although Tyson managed to land a few of his signature uppercuts.

Tyson was wobbled by a chopping right during the fifth round.

Soon, Tyson's left eye began to swell from Douglas' right jabs, preventing him from seeing his opponent's punches well.

In the eighth round, Douglas dominated until the last few seconds.

Within the last ten seconds of the round, Tyson, who had been backed onto the ropes, landed a big right uppercut that sent Douglas to the canvas.

Douglas rose as the referee signalled nine, but the bell ended the round.

In the ninth round, Tyson came out aggressively to try to end the fight and save his title, hoping that Douglas was still hurt from the eighth-round knockdown.

Douglas was able to fight off Tyson's attack.

Both men traded punches before Douglas connected on a four-punch combination that staggered Tyson back to the ropes.

With Tyson hurt along the ropes, Douglas closed in and unleashed a four-punch attack to try to knock Tyson out.

Tyson withstood the punishment and barely survived the ninth round.

In the tenth round, Tyson pushed forward, but he was still seriously hurting from the accumulation of punishment he had absorbed throughout the match.

As Tyson advanced, Douglas measured him with a few jabs before landing an uppercut that snapped Tyson's head upward, stopping Tyson in his tracks.

As Tyson reeled back, Douglas immediately followed with four punches to the head, knocking Tyson down for the first time in his career.

In a famous scene, Tyson fumbled for his mouthpiece on the canvas before sticking one end in his mouth with the other end hanging out.

The champion attempted to make it back to his feet, but the referee counted him out.

Buster Douglas thus became the new undisputed heavyweight champion, engineering one of the biggest upsets in boxing history.

When Douglas was interviewed after, he was asked how he did it.

And here's what happened.

When Douglas got the fight, he was so proud, and he went around telling people and his mum found out and his mum started telling everyone.

His mom was in hospital at the time.

And Douglas went to go and see his mum, his mum had been going, "Oh my god, my son's going to beat Mike Tyson."

She wasn't saying that her son had got a fight with Tyson, which was a feat in of itself, she was telling people that her son was going to win!

So Douglas made a vocal commitment and said, "That's what I'm going to do for you mum".

Not long before the fight, his mum died.

But he made that vocal commitment and that's what allowed him to keep on getting up.

His language created a new reality.

And when I say that, I mean that he took one of the hardest punches of all time from Mike Tyson and he was able to get back up.

He'd created a new belief, and it became a possibility.

For me, it was when I met John Reese for the first time.

He was one of the first people to make over a million in less than twenty-four hours online.

That just completely changed my whole view on what was possible because John had done it.

I knew it was possible.

Now it didn't happen overnight, that's for sure, but when I did it, I did a million in less than seven months.

I wrote about it in my book Coaching Business Secrets which you can get here: www.coachingbusinesssecrets.co.uk.

Off the back of that I ended up winning a Two Comma Club Award from ClickFunnels and I got flown out to meet Russell Brunson who owns ClickFunnels.

His business does as over a hundred million a year.

Your beliefs change who you are and who you spend time with.

And who you spend time with is who you become based on belief transference.

Beliefs can be transferred at lightning speed in exchange of a simple conversation or a story.

"Who you spend time with is who you become" is not a new concept.

The six people that you spend your time with are going to dictate your thinking, your stories, and your beliefs.

If your six people are stressed and anxious and invest into drama, they will reflect in your thinking, your stories, and your beliefs.

If your six people are overweight, eat in a certain way and do not value health, then this will reflect in your thinking, your stories, and your beliefs.

If your six people are all divorced, this will reflect in your thinking, your stories, and your beliefs.

If your closest six people you spend time with earn 23,000, which is the average salary, this will reflect in your thinking, in your stories, and in your beliefs.

And so the goal is, if you want higher levels of thinking, you need higher levels of beliefs.

The quickest way to get that is to get around people that are doing bigger stuff than you.

Therefore, if you can get into the circles where people are believing in more and doing more, that will correlate directly to your success.

The belief will drive the story.

The story drives the belief.

Which one comes first, it doesn't really matter.

Alter the **Story** - You alter the **Belief**

Alter the **Belief** - You alter the **Story**

Alter the story, you alter the belief.

Alter the belief, you alter the story.

And of course, we're altering the disempowered belief and the disempowered story.

And so, all that matters is the statement which your client says.

Notice when it's empowering versus disempowering.

Chapter 25

BREAKING DISEMPOWERING STORIES

Remember, if you lack diagnosis of the problem, then new problems occur because the core belief that created the problem in the first place is still held.

Thus a negative empowerment, a disempowering belief, will occur.

As will frustration occur.

The problem then strengthens, and disempowering emotions build.

Regression then occurs and the client continues to get worse.

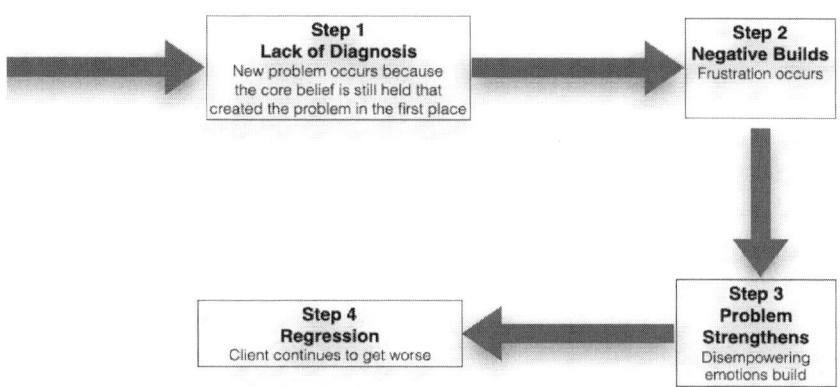

What we want to do is diagnose and understand how the belief structures the problem.

And then break it.

Once we break the core belief that creates the problem, then we're going to retrain that new belief so it doesn't progress and then we're going to move them into compounding so that they progress with new habits to create a new behaviour.

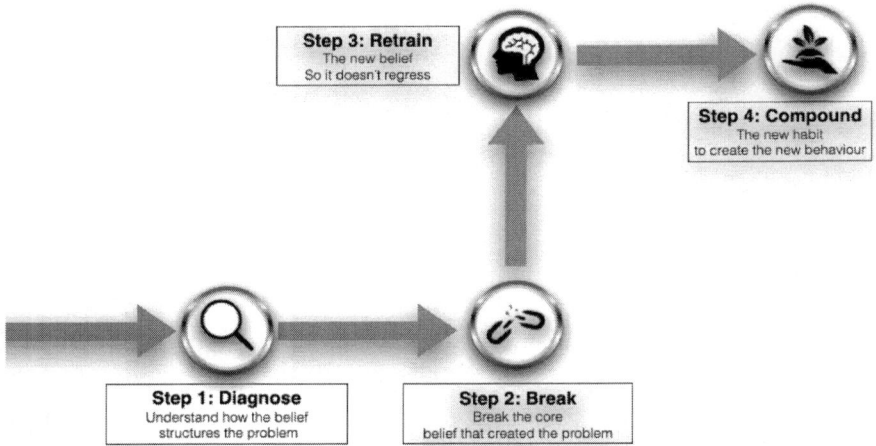

Language creates reality.

When someone says that "this means that", we have to understand that there is a belief underneath that.

The meaning is the story they tell themselves and within the story is the belief pattern that we want to break.

The best way to get this is to go out there in the world and hear these.

You have to listen to your client, collect your experience, and practice this process.

In the meantime, consider, "What is a thought?"

Could you describe what "a thought" is?

And while you consider that, also consider, "How does the brain find answers to problems?", which is what you are doing now.

The brain works through simply stimulating questions.

So a thought is a question.

And as you get into your meditation, you'll start to notice that you can catch those thoughts, you can catch those questions.

So by simply understanding questions, we start to understand how the brain creates reality.

There are 14 questions that create new meanings.

Now, you don't have to use these in every single session, and the goal is not to just read them out lineal, but you'll start to understand that you can pick your favourite ones.

You don't have to use them at the same time, and not all of these are going to be relevant to all statements, but you'll get comfortable with using them in time.

In time, you'll start to know what questions are best suited for when.

And here they are:

1. Question the truth.
2. Question the non-truth.
3. Question the truth for everyone.
4. Question if they applied it to themselves.
5. Question the time period on the view.
6. Question comparison based on values of importance.
7. Question the consequence.
8. Question the outcome.
9. Question the metaphorical view.
10. Question the altering view of the belief on the belief.
11. Question the details by getting specific and chunking down.
12. Question the purpose by chunking up.
13. Question a counter example.
14. Question the intent behind the statement.

Those are all the 14 questions.

As I said, you don't have to use all of them, but test all of them so you understand what sort of responses you get.

The goal is to work on the statement so that we break the meaning and open up a new meaning because a new meaning creates a new belief.

I had a client once who thought that, because their partner had liked someone else's picture on Instagram, that it "meant" that they were going to cheat on them.

So I took them through the 14 questions to open up different realities off the back of the questions.

1. I questioned the truth.
   "How do you know that that's true?"
   "When someone likes a post, is it not that they are just liking a post?"
2. I questioned the non-truth.

"How do you know it's not true?"

"How do you know that because they like the post, it means that they will cheat?"

3. I questioned if it was true for everyone.

"Is it true for everyone's view?"

"It may mean that in someone's view, but is it true for everyone?"

4. I questioned if they applied it to themselves.
   "Have you liked someone's picture and not cheated with them?"
5. I question the time period on the view.
   I put the view out into the future by asking, "What if in the future nothing happened?"

6. I question the comparison based on values of importance.
   I questioned the higher criteria values that they held by asking, "Is it important to stay true to a core value which is supporting content that you like?"

7. I questioned the consequence.
   "What happens if you continue to think like this?"
   "What happens if they comment?"
   "What happens if you stop someone from connecting with someone that they will want to connect with?"

8. I questioned the outcome.
   "What is another outcome that can shift this?"
   "Whether you believe it's bad or good, it's not as important as we find a higher agreement to the situation that we are dealing with right now. Is it important to allow someone freedom to express themselves as they feel."

9. I question the metaphorical view.
   I actually told a story in a different context with a different meaning.
   "I like someone's picture because I'm friends with them and as a result we did a business agreement together. Is that wrong?"

10. I questioned the altering view of the belief on the belief.
    "What other meaning could this mean?"
    "If liking a picture is cheating, is talking to someone cheating? Is thinking of someone else cheating?"
    "How is anyone going to live with this belief?"

11. I questioned the details by getting specific and chunking down.
    "What specifically? Give me examples of this?"
    "How do they cheat specifically?"

12. I questioned the purpose by chunking up.
    "For what purpose?"
    "Is it not the attention that is important?"
    "Are you giving attention to them?"

I questioned the purpose, and who wants the attention.

13. I questioned a counter example.

Here I inverted it in on itself - when is there a time when A doesn't cause B?

"Is it possible to like a picture and not cheat?"

"Is it possible to not like a picture and cheat?"

14. I questioned the intent behind the statement.

Here I questioned whether they are saying this for their secondary gain.

"Do you want them to like your picture? Would that change your life?"

The only way to get good of this is just to write these down, listen to the client and practice them.

Let's run this through on the statement I heard from a client once, "Saying bad things means you're a bad person."

1. I questioned the truth.

"How do you know that that's true?"

"Is it not true that what one perceived as bad could be good?"

"And if that is true, sometimes our worst experiences become our best experiences. So does bad really exist?"

2. I questioned the non-truth.

"How do you know it's not true?"

"How do you know that saying bad things means that you're a bad person?"

3. I questioned if it was true for everyone.

"Is it true for everyone's view?"

"Everyone?" "Always?" "Never?"

"It may seem mean in your view of the world, however in some views of the world, this is how we show that we care for one another."

4. I questioned if they applied it to themselves.

   "Is that not a mean thing to say?"

   "Saying bad things means you're a bad person. Is that not a mean thing to say?"

5. I question the time period on the view.

   I put the view out into the future by asking, "It may seem bad, however in the long run could it be a good thing?"

6. I question the comparison based on values of importance.

   "Isn't it more important to fulfil one duty to serve you at the highest value and that sometimes to do that we'll have to say some things that you may not want to hear?"

   "Is it not more important to serve one's [insert their highest value of importance] than being nice in this moment?"

7. I questioned the consequence.

   "What happens if you continue to think like this?"

   "If one hadn't have said that, then would it not be that they've not been displaying their truth as they view it?"

   "I totally respect your view. However, the consequence of being stuck in a fixed view can mean that you're missing valuable insights from another side of this."

   "I wouldn't want you to be at disadvantage at later stages as a direct result from this."

   "I only say these things to make you better."

8. I questioned the outcome.

   "What is another outcome that can shift this?"

   "Whether you believe it's bad or good, it's not as important as we find a higher agreement to the situation that we are dealing with right now."

9. I question the metaphorical view.

   I told a story in a different context with a different meaning.

   "Nelson Mandela caused bad things to happen whilst he was creating a new shift in a global way in which the world thought at that time. He said things that some didn't want to hear. However, what occurred was a new level of thinking. Does that make him a bad person?"

10. I questioned the altering view of the belief on the belief.

    "What other meaning could this equation have?"

    "They are not bad, it's just you don't like how this sounds from your view and that's okay."

    "We don't have to agree on everything to be friends, do we?"

    "It's not that I don't care or that I'm a bad person, it's that I am willing to say things that you are not comfortable hearing because it's different to your view and how you perceive the world."

11. I questioned the details by getting specific and chunking down.

    "Bad? How specifically?"

12. I questioned the purpose by chunking up.

    "For what purpose?"

    "Are you saying that being a good person is based on just things they say?"

    "Are there more important aspects of life to consider?"

13. I questioned a counter example.

    "Is it possible to say bad things and be a good person?"

    "Is it possible to say good things and be a bad person?"

14. I questioned the intent behind the statement.

"My intention was purely to say it as I saw it so that it would help you to see a different view point."

"My intention is never to upset you or to make you feel a certain way that is uncomfortable because I care."

Action

Write out all 14 questions by hand.

Chapter 26

THE BELIEF BREAKING SCRIPT

To go alongside the statement breaking questions we covered in the previous chapter, below in The Belief Breaking Script.

Now this could be in one breakthrough session, or you could break it up into parts.

I recommend that you focus on a core belief.

Once we find a core belief then, the truth is, the rest fall down like dominoes.

But there has to be some adaptability here.

So when you're using it in the context of your session, you're going to be taking the script and you're going to be asking your client to reply back.

It's a powerful tool because it helps your client to challenge and modify negative or irrational beliefs that hold them back.

What is the belief you'd like to break?

....

If it's ok, can you close your eyes, relax, reflect and witness what you see.

Is the belief true? [Pause]

Can you absolutely know that it's true? [Pause]

Does it make sense that for something to be absolutely true it has to be true ALL the time.

When you believe " .... " what images do you see when you believe that thought? How do you react when you believe that thought, what happens? How do you feel emotionally?

....

....

....

How have you failed to resolve this belief?

How can you overcome the solution to your belief?

a

....

b (How else?)

....

Keep your eyes closed and continue to relax.

Would you impose this very same belief on someone you loved?

[PAUSE]

Would you be happy if someone close to you were to internalise this belief?

[PAUSE]

Tell me, how would you want that person you loved to change? What do you want them to do?

....

In this situation, what advice would you offer them?

....

Now, as you think about your present situation in life, notice how many options you have, now. You want to make changes, haven't you ...

What could you be doing if you weren't holding on to this belief?

....

Give me an example of what you could easily do differently if you didn't have that belief?

a

....

b (What else?)

....

c (if you were to know, what else?)

....

Who or what are you without the belief?

....

So let's reverse the belief.

Change it to "..............................."

What would it be like when you have made those changes, now? [PAUSE]

In the future, as you look back and see what it was like to have had that belief, as you think about it now, if you could make this change for yourself so that you could STOP NOW having made that change and see yourself now.

Do you like the way you look now that you've changed that belief and look back at yourself having made that change now!

[PAUSE]
This new belief is as true or truer than the original belief, isn't it, yes!

So, when you think of that old belief, just notice how you feel now.

Notice how many ways you know you have solved this. I know you are changing and seeing things differently.

And as you think about the next time you may believe it, knowing what you know now, notice how much better you feel, not doing it.

The belief-breaking script is a powerful tool that can help individuals to challenge and modify negative beliefs, promote positive thinking, address cognitive distortions, promote self-awareness, and provide a practical framework for change.

Action

Take someone you know through The Belief Breaking Script.

RETRAINING

Chapter 27

THE CHAMPION CODE SYSTEM

So far we have Diagnosed how the reality of the problem was create and Broken the belief that structures the problem.

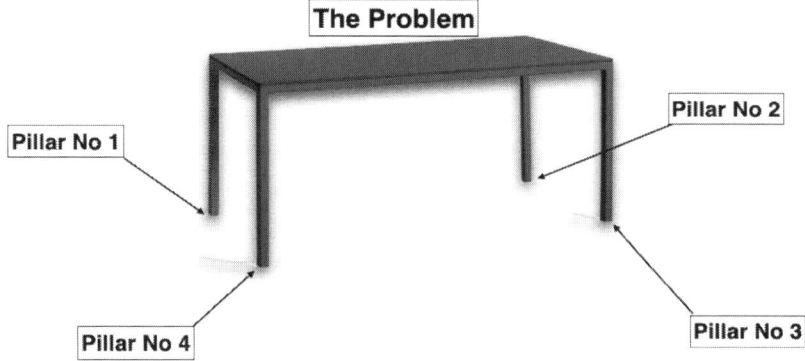

Now we move onto Pillar 3 which is Retraining the behaviour so the problem doesn't create somewhere else.

Remember, the 7 key areas that condition beliefs are:

- Environment
- Parents
- Education
- Social Groups
- Experiences
- Repetition
- Impact

Retraining conditioned beliefs is important because our beliefs shape our thoughts, emotions, and behaviours, and ultimately determine the decisions we make and the actions we take.

Our beliefs are not always based on accurate information or evidence, and they can be influenced by many factors, including our upbringing, culture, environment, and experiences.

Conditioned beliefs are those that have been learned through repeated exposure to certain ideas or experiences.

They can be deeply ingrained and may not always align with reality or with our current values and goals.

Retraining conditioned beliefs can help us to break free from limiting or harmful patterns of thinking and behaviour and to develop new, more positive and empowering beliefs that better serve our needs and aspirations.

By retraining conditioned beliefs, we can expand our perspective, challenge our assumptions, and become more open-minded and adaptable.

This can help us to improve our relationships, achieve our goals, and lead a more fulfilling and satisfying life.

In addition, as we encounter new information and experiences throughout our lives, our beliefs will naturally evolve and change.

Being willing and able to retrain our beliefs as needed can help us to stay current, relevant, and effective in an ever-changing world.

We must retrain the beliefs with a new code.

Retraining beliefs with new code requires a deliberate and intentional process of identifying and examining your client's current beliefs, understanding the new code that challenges those beliefs, and then actively working to help the client integrate and adopt the new beliefs.

We do this by allowing our client to be stimulated by new touch points.

New touch points equal new codes.

The CHAMPION Code System is a touch point system.

C - Care – Care what they care about. Care about what's important to them and why.

H – Honesty – What do they honestly want? What is the truth as they see it?

A – Action – What is the cost of not taking action on that? (This is the logical)

M – Motivation – How do they feel about that? (This is the emotional)

P – People – How does this impact on their most important people? (This is the social pressure)

I – Inspiration – What is the impact of taking this actual step that you're helping them do? (This is the forward pace – imagining it happening)

O – Observational – This is disassociated feedback from both the client and the coach. So they look back now at seeing themselves doing this thing. The brain starts to imagine this is happening. And then you look back and you start to see it happening.

N – Never Give Up – A commitment on the one action step to take forward.

That is The CHAMPION Code System.

Questions To Use In The Champion Code System

C – Caring

What do you care about right most now? Being? Love? Energy? Impact?

Pick one and focus on it until an improvement occurs.

H – Honesty

What is the problem as you see it?

How is that a problem?

How long has it been a problem?

Notice are they are not being honest.

Question the truth of the problem to assess the belief underneath the problem.

Call out anything dishonest and bring awareness to this so they can be their truth.

A – Action

Bring awareness to the cost of action.

What is this costing you?

Are you aware of what this is costing you?

How much has this cost you already? Emotionally? Financially? With friends and family?

What is it costing you to not have the thing that you want?

M – Motivation

Move them to an emotional decision.

How does that make you feel when you're losing that cost?

How do you want to feel instead?

P – People

What does this impact on?

How does it impact on other people?

Who do you want to do this for?

Why do you want to do it with them?

And what will this do for you?

I – Inspirational

If you can take this step, what will this allow for you?

What will this do for others in your life?

What will this do for your mission?

So you're moving them to an inspirational step.

O – Observational

Be observation around how to take this on.

Notice if you think that they will follow through or not.

Call out what you observe.

Ask them to observe the situation.

So you're really saying, "Can you see yourself doing it?"

Do you see yourself doing this and following through?

N – Never Give Up

Get a solid commitment; by when are they going to do it?

When are we going to do this thing?

Put a date in there.

Remember, changing beliefs takes time and effort.

Be patient with yourself and give yourself the space to learn and grow.

Action

Write out The Champion Code System by hand.

COMPOUNDING

Chapter 28

THE POWER OF COMPOUNDING

Pillar 4, Compounding, brings it all together.

We have Diagnosed how the reality of the problem was created.

We have Broken the belief that structures the problem.

We have Retrained the behaviour so the problem doesn't create somewhere else.

Now we are Compounding daily behaviours that allow a new empowering behaviour to grow.

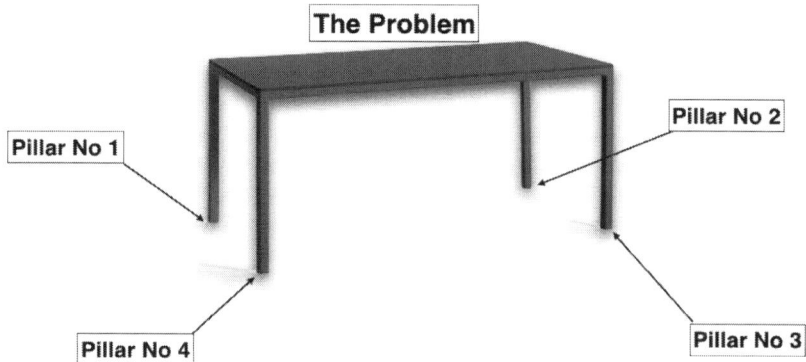

Remember, you can't do all of this in one session, which is why your clients will be coming to you for eight-to-twelve-week periods and beyond.

What compounding does is reinforces for your client what is important to them.

We use the power of compounding 1%, the goal being to make them 1% better each time.

We don't need to make them 100% better in one session.

Instead, we focus our client on improving just 1% daily.

We focus them on one step at a time.

One door at a time.

1% progression each time.

If we can do that every session, we will take the client into a whole different world.

1% better each day equated to 37 times better over the course of a year.

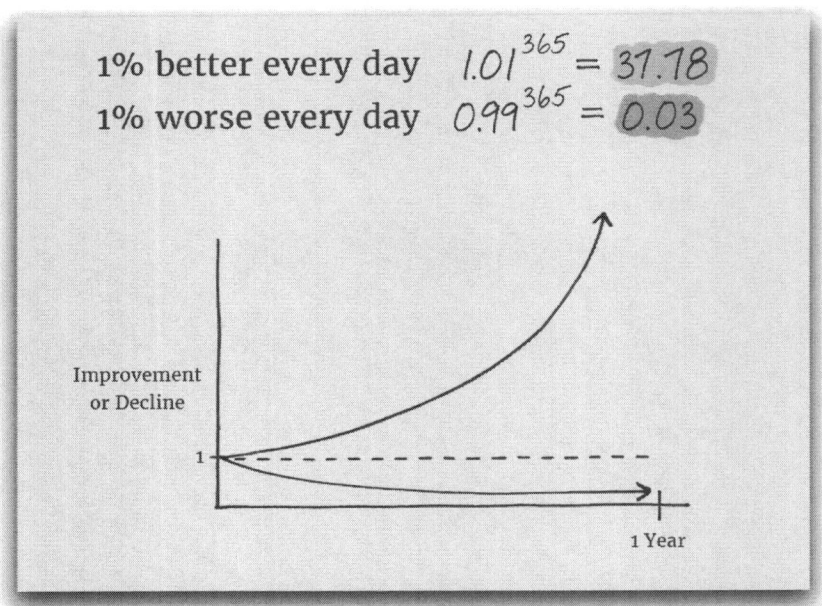

So if you and your clients improve 1% each day then you will be 37 times better then you used to be at the end a year.

138

By the time you get to the Compounding Pillar, you have Diagnosed and written down your client's statements.

Then you are questioning those statements to break the belief.

You could take them through The Belief Breaking Script of just individually question their statements.

From here you're Retraining, picking something they really care about from The Sacred 4.

Your role here is to focus your client on completing actions that they want to achieve on, and then hold them accountable to those actions.

This is designed around your client specifically, so you are adapting to their needs.

Design their 1 step.

Design their 1 door.

Design their 1%.

AFTERWORD

Chapter 29

NEVER GIVE UP

My first ever job was as a cleaner at the local gym.

After working my way up to being a personal trainer, I started helping women with weight loss workouts.

At first, most of those women failed to lose weight and eventually quit.

It broke my heart because I desperately wanted to help.

So I studied the few women who did stick to their plans and meet their goals...

...and they all had something BIG in common:

They'd simply had ENOUGH.

And their mindset wasn't that they were on a temporary "diet" and exercise plan...

Instead, they made the decision to make a lifestyle change...

And DO everything they needed to DO to become healthier.

Because there's no way around it...

For any of us...

We have to BE a thin person in a fat person's body BEFORE we can be slim in real life.

Does that make sense?

And it's the same with coaching.

We have to BE the coach we really want to be...

...and DO everything that version of ourselves would do...

...BEFORE we get there.

Back when I first got started coaching...

For me that meant investing heavily in my own education and mentoring as a coach.

Because, guess what?

ALL the successful people I saw online and wanted to emulate...well, they all invested thousands every year in coaches, mentors and masterminds.

So I realised if I wanted to get to that level...I had to BE at that level.

I was also at the stage where I wanted to charge high ticket prices for my coaching...

...but I hadn't even invested in MYSELF at that level yet.

I was in-congruent with myself. And my (poor) results showed.

But everything changed when I started investing in myself and acting like "Future Successful Ed" NOW... even though on the outside I was still "Normal Ed" :-)

Many coaches struggle with sales because they lack congruence.

They're out of alignment and it hangs around like a bad smell even if they don't realise it.

It's hard to hold others to account if you can't hold yourself to account.

It's hard to help others with transformation unless you've experienced transformation yourself.

And it's almost impossible to charge high ticket prices unless you've paid high ticket prices yourself.

It's much easier to start hitting consistent 5k, 10k even 20k months when you've made a leap of faith in yourself.

When YOU change, your business changes too.